TRUMPETS

by Pamela K. Harris

The Child's World®
childsworld.com

Published by The Child's World®
1980 Lookout Drive • Mankato, MN 56003-1705
800-599-READ • www.childsworld.com

Design element: Vector memory/Shutterstock.com
Photo credits: alexandre zveiger/Shutterstock.com: 12; Amirul Syaidi/Shutterstock.com: 17; Chromakey/
Shutterstock.com: 21 (French horn and trombone); DenisProduction.com/Shutterstock.com: 11;
furtseff/Shutterstock.com: 7, 8; Horatiu Bota/Shutterstock.com: 21 (flügelhorn and pocket trumpet);
Howard Sandler/Shutterstock.com: 7; Mikalai Kachanovich/Shutterstock.com: 4; PhotoHouse/
Shutterstock.com: 18; Sashkin/Shutterstock.com: 21 (bugle); Sideways Design/Shutterstock.
com: cover, 1; tobkatrina/Shutterstock.com: 14; the palms/Shutterstock.com: 21 (tuba)

ISBN: 9781503831919
LCCN: 2018960415

Printed in the United States of America
PA02417

Table *of* Contents

CHAPTER ONE

The Trumpet

The king is coming! Trumpets blare the news. Long ago, trumpets were played for kings and queens. Their special sound grew to be loved by almost everyone who heard it.

The sound of a trumpet is still loved today. Instead of just being played for royalty, trumpets are played almost everywhere. Trumpets belong to a group of instruments called **wind instruments**. Wind instruments make sounds when air is blown through them. Flutes and trombones are wind instruments, too.

❮ *Herald trumpets like this one are long, skinny, and straight.*

CHAPTER TWO

Different Kinds of Trumpets

Trumpets are very old instruments. In fact, some trumpets were even discovered in a pyramid in Egypt! One trumpet was made of silver. Another was made of bronze.

"Embouchure" (AHM-boo-shur) is the word for a musician's lips on a trumpet.

Long ago, most trumpets were made from reeds, horns, or shells. Since they could make such loud noises, trumpets were often used for celebrations. Today, most trumpets are made of brass.

A shofar is a type of trumpet that has been used for thousands of years. Shofars are made from animal horns. ❯

CHAPTER THREE

Brass Instruments

There are two types of instruments in the wind instrument group. **Woodwinds** have lots of holes that musicians must open and close with their fingertips. Covering each hole changes the woodwind's sound.

Brass instruments are usually made of metal. They have **valves** to move the air in different directions. This changes the instrument's sound. Some brass instruments have parts that slide in and out to change the sound. Trumpets belong to the brass group.

❮ *Players use their right hand to press buttons that control the valves.*

CHAPTER FOUR

The Shape

Trumpets from long ago looked very different from the ones we know today. The oldest trumpets were just a straight tube that widened at the end. These instruments were very long and heavy. People had to rest one end on the ground to play them!

To make trumpets easier to play, instrument makers began to bend the tube of the trumpet. Over time, the tube became even more curved. Today, the tube part of a trumpet looks like a flattened letter S.

Can you see this trumpet's S shape?. ❯

CHAPTER FIVE

Parts of the Trumpet

A trumpet is a hollow tube with a **mouthpiece** on one end and a flared **bell** on the other. The bell makes the sound louder—like cupping your hands around your mouth.

Stretched out, a trumpet has more than 6 feet (1 m) of tubing.

Sometimes the bell end is blocked with a mute. The mute changes the **volume** and **tone** of the sounds the trumpet makes. It makes the trumpet play quieter and with a softer sound.

❮ *There are hooks and loops on a trumpet for your fingers. These help you grip the instrument.*

CHAPTER SIX

Playing the Trumpet

To play a trumpet, you put your lips on the mouthpiece and make them **vibrate** as you blow. You have to blow so that the air goes into the tube. Don't let any air escape from the sides of your mouth!

To play a trumpet, you buzz your lips together.

❮ *This trumpet player is blowing air into the mouthpiece.*

CHAPTER SEVEN

The Valves

Valves change the sounds or notes a trumpet can make. Pushing a valve down forces the air through a side tube. It travels around, comes back through the main tube, and goes out through the bell. Making the air travel around—rather than directly through the bell—changes the sound. This is how a trumpet makes different notes.

The valves move up and down to make different notes. ❯

CHAPTER EIGHT

Jazz Trumpet

The trumpet is often played in jazz music. Louis Armstrong was one of the greatest trumpet players of all time. He was one of the first jazz trumpeters to play **solo**, or by himself. Dizzy Gillespie and Miles Davis were also famous trumpet players.

Jazz music started in New Orleans in the late 1800s.

❮ *Wynton Marsalis is another famous jazz trumpet player.*

Index

About the Author

Pamela K. Harris grew up in Oregon and currently lives in Denver, Colorado. She directs a non-profit organization that provides early childhood education to children from low-income backgrounds. She has testified before Congress on the importance of early childhood education. She loves being a student herself and has a PhD in Educational Leadership.